P

# *Hosea*

## THE LOVE THAT NEVER FAILS

**CWR**

Selwyn Hughes
with Ian Sewter

Copyright © CWR 2004

Published 2004 by CWR, Waverley Abbey House, Waverley Lane, Farnham, Surrey GU9 8EP, UK. Registered Charity No. 294387. Registered Limited Company No. 1990308. Reprinted 2010, 2013, 2019.

Text taken from *Every Day with Jesus*, 'The Love that Never Fails' July/August 1997 by Selwyn Hughes. Adaptation and additional material by Ian Sewter.

The right of Ian Sewter to be identified as the coauthor of this work has been asserted by him in accordance with the Copyright, Designs and Patents Act 1988, sections 77 and 78.

For list of National Distributors, visit cwr.org.uk/distributors

Unless otherwise indicated, all Scripture references are from the Holy Bible: New International Version (NIV), copyright © 1973, 1978, 1984 by the International Bible Society.

Concept development, editing, design and production by CWR.

Front cover image: Roger Walker.

Printed in the UK by Linney.

ISBN: 978-1-85345-290-1

# Contents

# Introduction

There is in every human heart a deep longing to be loved. We are designed to be loved; built for it. And we long to be loved consistently – to be loved with a love that will never be taken away. The prophecy of Hosea introduces us to exactly that kind of love – a love that goes on loving despite all the frailties and weaknesses in the one who is loved. This undying love for which we all long can only be found in the heart of the deity. However we see something of the same degree of love in the heart of Hosea who, commanded by God to marry a prostitute, keeps on loving her despite her adulterous ways.

In the introductory verse of his prophecy we see that Hosea's ministry covers the time of several significant kings who reigned at various stages of the eighth century BC. It was a time of spiritual decline and decadence in Israel. Jeroboam II of Israel and his contemporary, Uzziah of Judah, were close to the end of their long reigns. In the distance, the great nation of Assyria was gathering strength and would soon march on Palestine. Israel was a generation away from being overwhelmed. It was at such a time that the word of the Lord came to Hosea. The command that came to Hosea to take to himself a wife who was promiscuous is one of the most astonishing charges that ever came from the lips of the Almighty. Usually when people think of marriage they have in mind someone who is moral, respectable and well established in society. But the person God had in mind for Hosea was a local prostitute. Not the most welcome engagement announcement, you might think. Why would God lead one of His choice servants into such a situation? The answer is found in the latter half of the text of Hosea 1:2 'because the land is guilty of the vilest adultery'.

Years previously, Israel had entered into a covenant with the almighty when she promised to be faithful to Him:

'We will do everything the LORD has said; we will obey'
(Exod. 24:7). The vow they made that day was similar to a
marriage vow. God and Israel were joined together in an
indissoluble union. To mark the occasion God gave Israel the
Ten Commandments and the message implicit in this was,
'Keep these – and we will live happily ever after.' It was not
long, however, before Israel had broken every one of the Ten
Commandments and God appeared to leave her to her own
devices. But divine love is a persistent love. God used another
approach when He asked Hosea to help Him act out before
the whole nation a powerful real-life drama that might help
bring home to Israel the lesson she sorely needed to learn.
'Help me, Hosea,' the Almighty seems to be saying. 'I have a
marriage problem. Israel is my bride but she is unfaithful to
me. Marry a prostitute. Love her as I love Israel. Perhaps she
will see in your actions a picture of my own undying love.'

We must remember, as we go through the book of Hosea,
that both Israel and Gomer are in the same frame. The story
of Israel is the story of Gomer – and vice versa. We should
continually remind ourselves, as we make our way through
the chapters of Hosea's powerful prophecy, that the central
motif of the book is that of an unfaithful bride and a faithful
bridegroom. God is married to Israel and is passionately
concerned that their marriage becomes a success. Love, after
all, is what marriage is all about, and when love is lost or
unrequited the marriage is an empty shell. It is bad enough
living with a bride who has wandering affections, but to live
with one who is actively engaged in prostitution is one of the
hardest situations imaginable. But God's love, as we know, is a
tough love and He enters upon a course of action which at first
looks petulant but is designed to show His bride the folly of
her behaviour and win her back to His side.

Can there be a happy ending for Israel? Yes, there can. Following repentance, her life will not just be a bed of roses but of blossoming flowers! 'I will heal their way-wardness and love them freely... [and] be like the dew to Israel; [s]he will blossom like a lily' (14:4–5). Israel had discarded God a long time ago and thus is as dry and arid as a desert, but one day God will come raining down on the Israelites so that Israel's 'splendour will be like an olive tree, his fragrance like a cedar of Lebanon'. Israel will no longer have the cheap smell of a prostitute but have about her the perfume of God. She will also be as fruitful in her love as the fruitful vineyards are with grapes. God's love wins in the end!

WEEK ONE

# A love that will not let go

### Opening Icebreaker

What do you love and enjoy in terms of interests, friendships, food, pets, possessions etc. How have you felt when these pleasures have been denied through ill health, theft or other circumstances? Having sworn to uphold the law, how would a judge or policeman feel if they discovered their child was a drug dealer?

### Bible Reading

• Hosea 1:1–2:23

## Opening Our Eyes

It is one thing to preach a sermon; it is another thing to live it. What God was asking of Hosea was to enter into a marriage that seemed destined to fail. Most men, when they propose marriage, have high expectations for their future but Hosea thought from the start that his marriage was doomed. How could God treat one of His faithful servants in this way? The Almighty knew that in Hosea He had someone who would put the divine interest before his own interests – someone who would not baulk at the idea of sacrificing his own comfort for the greater good. If at first this seems to make God out to be cold and uncaring then take my word for it – that is not the case. The Almighty had tried every way possible to save His marriage to the nation of Israel, but nothing had succeeded. There was no other way than for Hosea to put himself in a position where his abiding love for a promiscuous woman would become a visual aid to an equally promiscuous nation.

Things may be difficult between God and His people but God does not forget His vow and repeats it here with conviction. Judgment is not God's last word – love is. The divine heart will seek to save the marriage despite all the hurt, anguish and pain. Just like a frustrated husband, God expresses His hurt and anger toward His unfaithful bride but then lets her know that, despite all His exasperation, He takes His marriage vows seriously and will work toward constructing a way of reconciliation and restoration. Infidelity in a marriage is a terrible and hurtful thing. Some reading these lines might be caught up in that discovery and there is nothing wrong with feeling hurt and angry. I know some Christians who think that allowing feelings of hurt and anger to rise in the heart is unspiritual and thus, even though they are there, they pretend they don't have them. This is foolish. Unacknowledged emotions cause trouble. You don't have to act on them but you do have to acknowledge them.

God acknowledged His feelings of frustration and anger but then He brought to mind His previous promise of commitment and proceeded to act – not on His feelings but on what He knew was right. That is the divine way. With God's help it must be ours too.

The main thrust of the second chapter is God's complaint against Israel in terms of the analogy of the marriage covenant. Most commentators take the view that whilst God is unfolding the story of Israel's adultery the same kind of thing is happening to Hosea and Gomer, and thus Israel and Gomer are to be seen in parallel. For 'Israel' read 'Gomer'.

The Almighty may be pained when His people go astray but He is never seen as wringing His hands in despair. Divine concern must never be interpreted as self-pity. How reassuring it is to know that God is not against us for our sin but for us against our sin. Or, to put it in a more familiar way – He hates sin, but loves the sinner.

Why should God go to such endless lengths to win back His bride? There is only one answer – love. Not pity, not the urge to show He cannot be beaten. Not even the desire to overcome sin. It is love; sheer unadulterated, inextinguishable love. A love that simply will not let go.

## Discussion Starters

1. How does the story of Hosea demonstrate obedience?

   _____

   _____

   _____

2. How does the story of Hosea demonstrate disobedience?

   _____

   _____

   _____

3. Why may God's discipline be reassuring?

   _____

   _____

   _____

4. How were the attitudes of Gomer and Israel linked?

   _____

   _____

   _____

5. How were the attitudes of Hosea and God linked?

   _____

   _____

   _____

**6.** What does the word 'covenant' mean?

_____

_____

_____

**7.** Describe God's feelings about His people.

_____

_____

_____

**8.** What were Israel's transgressions?

_____

_____

_____

**9.** How does God combine judgment and mercy? Which is more important?

_____

_____

_____

**10.** Why does love cause both joy and pain?

_____

_____

_____

## Personal Application

How often we read that in the Old Testament a crisis forms, and God meets it by giving a word to someone.

Are you facing a crisis in your life at this time? A financial collapse, a broken relationship, a marriage difficulty, a set of circumstances that threaten to engulf you? I think God has something to say to you in the days ahead. The word that God gave Hosea is a word for you. God loves you and will keep on loving you no matter what. His love surpasses the highest of human loves. It is a love that never lets go. None of us has drifted so far from God that there is no way back because 'He is patient with you, not wanting anyone to perish, but everyone to come to repentance' (2 Pet. 3:9). Remember also, however, that when God spoke, Hosea appeared not to hesitate or negotiate but simply obeyed. Hosea knew that the first rule of loving God is – obedience. Our fellowship with God rises and falls at the point of obedience (1 John 2:3–6).

## Seeing Jesus in the Scriptures

Jesus was obedient to His Father even though it meant both relinquishing the glory of heaven and His death on the cross (Phil. 2:1–8). Jesus not only proved His great love by dying for His friends (John 15:13) but that love also led Him to die for His enemies and seek forgiveness for those who crucified Him (Luke 23:34). Even after Peter denied Him, Jesus sought Peter out to restore him to full relationship once again (John 21:15–19).

WEEK TWO

# A love that is out of this world

## Opening Icebreaker

What examples of sacrificial love can you think of from human experience or the world of nature?

## Bible Reading

- Hosea 3:1–4:19

**Opening Our Eyes**

God commands the prophet to take again his adulterous wife and pick up their relationship where it had been left off. Note that Gomer was still living in an adulterous relationship: 'though she is loved by another' (3:1). This shows that her adultery had not been an isolated lapse but a desertion and the fact that she continued in her sin added insult to injury. One commentator describes the love that was asked of Hosea as 'heroic'. Another says, 'It was the kind of love that was out of this world.' That was exactly what it was meant to picture – a love out of this world. Hosea captures, as no other prophet does, the tremendous power of divine love – a love that goes on seeking to win the wandering heart back to Himself and refuses to give up. What pain there must be in a heart that loves like this. Yet, as Derek Kidner points out, the Divine Lover 'refuses to ease the pain of his relationship either by compromise or quitting'. All God had to do to stop the pain was to stop loving. But He just can't. He is love.

Doubtless when Hosea walked into the marketplace to buy back his bride from slavery, the gossipmongers would have watched and afterwards carried the story throughout the length and breadth of Israel. And the more they talked the more they spread the message that God wanted them to hear – the message of a love that never gives up. After Hosea pays the purchase price for his slave wife, the next question is: How is he going to piece together their broken relationship? Lesson No. 1: no sex. 'You shall be betrothed to me... you shall not play the harlot and you shall not belong to another man. So will I also be to you until you have proved your loyalty to me and our marital relations may be resumed' (3:3, Amplified Bible).

To Gomer, love was something merely physical. Hosea knew differently, however, and set about teaching her that love is more than sex and that sex is merely the expression of love. I think Hosea's reason for sexual abstinence was to attempt to teach her the difference between love and lust – love can always wait to give, lust can never wait to get.

No sooner has Hosea been reconciled to his wife than God commands him to bring charges against Israel and to act as His spokesman and advocate. Israel, as we have seen, refused to accept God as her one true Husband. She had violated her marriage vows and spent her wedding anniversaries flirting with other gods. The problem now ends up in the high court of heaven and charges are levelled against the unfaithful bride. The charge is breach of promise. The trial is soon over and the verdict is given – Israel is guilty.

Hosea, as the representative of the court of heaven, is to deliver the sentence. Who better? He has been prepared for this very moment. His marriage has been in trouble too. He loved his wife, was separated from her, endured the pain of her adulterous relationships and thus he can speak with true understanding. I picture him striding into the marketplace – perhaps the very marketplace where he bought Gomer back from slavery – and pronouncing God's word to the people. 'There is no faithfulness, no love, no acknowledgment [or knowledge] of God in the land,' says Hosea (4:1). But punishment is not the last word because after pruning comes blessings (Hosea 3:5). Lust simply punishes an unfaithful lover, true love seeks reconciliation and restoration.

## Discussion Starters

1. What are the characteristics of lust?

   _____
   _____
   _____

2. What are the characteristics of love?

   _____
   _____
   _____

3. Why is marriage more than sex?

   _____
   _____
   _____

4. Why does God not simply stop loving those who are unfaithful to Him?

   _____
   _____
   _____

5. What is the meaning of redemption and what does it mean for your own relationship with God?

   _____
   _____
   _____

**6.** What is the meaning of reconciliation and restoration?

_____

_____

_____

**7.** What is the process of genuine repentance?

_____

_____

_____

**8.** Why might people exchange the worship of God for idols?

_____

_____

_____

**9.** What part does the knowledge of God play in our relationship with Him and how is it obtained?

_____

_____

_____

**10.** Why is the nature of God's love out of this world?

_____

_____

_____

## Personal Application

These three things – faithfulness, love and knowledge – form the basis of any good and ongoing marital relationship; indeed, for that matter, of any developing relationship. God can only be known as a relationship with Him is cultivated and developed. And what He longs for above all – never forget this – is not simply the obedient acts of His people but a close relationship with them. Sin is never seen in its true light until it is seen not simply as violating certain rules and regulations but as damaging a relationship. And more is needed to rebuild a broken relationship than quick apologies and hasty resolutions. There is only one way – repentance. To repent means to rethink one's position, to realise one's foolishness and return to God with a sorrowful heart and a contrite spirit. Once we move away from God this is the only way back.

## Seeing Jesus in the Scriptures

The text of Romans 5:6–8 reads, 'You see, at just the right time, when we were still powerless, Christ died for the ungodly. Very rarely will anyone die for a righteous man, though for a good man someone might possibly dare to die. But God demonstrates his own love for us in this: While we were still sinners, Christ died for us.' Jesus gave His life not for people who were faithful to God but for those who had rejected God and sought the love of others and possessions instead of truly worshipping their creator. Christ's love for us was a love that was literally out of this world.

WEEK THREE

# An unrequited love

## Opening Icebreaker

What are some modern-day idols that people worship and seek instead of responding to God's love?

## Bible Reading

- Hosea 5:1–6:11

## Opening Our Eyes

The fundamental reason why the people of God chase after idols and flirt with other deities is because deep in their heart they lack a knowledge of God (5:4). The Amplified Version puts it like this: 'they do not recognize, appreciate, give heed to, or cherish the Lord.' When there is no personal knowledge of God, then religion becomes a matter of ceremony and rituals. We have a picture of people going through all the due process of religion and yet God is not listening to them. 'When they go with their flocks and herds to seek the LORD,' says Hosea, 'they will not find him' (5:6). How tragic. There was a similar situation described in another part of the Old Testament (Amos 8), when God said that if the people did not heed His word they would not hear His word, and they would experience a famine for the word of God. Nothing can be more terrible than to talk or plead with the Lord and for Him not to answer, but that is what may happen if we do not take God seriously. Hosea tells us also that the new moon festivals (see 1 Sam. 20:5–18 or Amos 8:5; Col. 2:16) – festivals designed to please God – were now offensive to Him. A dead formalism and religious ritual is no substitute for a living faith and loving relationship. Sacrifice and burnt offerings cannot replace mercy and true intimacy.

How sad and hurt God must feel when His people resort to every other means to save themselves rather than to humbly repent and turn to Him. The heart of the Almighty is in great pain as He ponders the fact of His bride's unrequited love. Listen as He cries out: 'What can I do with you, Ephraim? What can I do with you, Judah? Your love is like the morning mist, like the early dew that disappears' (6:4). Israel's love, like some weather reports, promised much but never delivered on the promises. Dawn in the ancient land of Palestine often brought promise. The mist would descend, bringing with it much needed moisture. But then the sun came out and quickly the mist would vanish in the warm air. The ground would soon be dry again. Israel's love was like that – it was long on promises but short on fulfilment.

In this section the Almighty pictures Himself as a lion, not defending His people but ravaging them. Ephraim and Judah, we are told, will turn for help to Assyria rather than to God, but their appeal will be in vain. God will discomfort them and ensure that they are not rescued; then He will withdraw like a lion to its lair, leaving them in distress. What is His purpose in all this? The text of Hosea 5:15 spells it out with great clarity: 'in their misery they will earnestly seek me.' It is a sad comment on our human condition that God sometimes has to make us miserable before we seek His face. This is what C. S. Lewis describes as a 'severe mercy' – God allowing difficult circumstances to come upon us in order to draw us more closely to Himself. Although the remedy is painful, its results are restorative. The Almighty loves His people too much to let them get away with things, and if necessary He will bring them down to misery in order that they will seek His face.

## Discussion Starters

1. What place should ceremony and ritual play in the Christian faith?

   _____

   _____

   _____

2. Why does God sometimes make His people miserable?

   _____

   _____

   _____

3. Why may an offering or prayers be unacceptable to God?

   _____

   _____

   _____

4. Why would God withdraw Himself from people who seek Him?

   _____

   _____

   _____

5. How can we ensure our love for God is not like the morning mist?

   _____

   _____

   _____

**6.** What are difficult circumstances designed to teach us?

_____

_____

_____

**7.** Why should people not take God's forgiveness
for granted?

_____

_____

_____

**8.** What is the difference between relationship, fellowship
and intimacy?

_____

_____

_____

**9.** Can you give examples of 'severe mercy'?

_____

_____

_____

## Personal Application

The spiritual and the social are much more intertwined than many realise. I wish some of our befuddled politicians would recognise this. Many of them say, 'What a man or woman does privately bears no relation to their work.' Doesn't it? If a man cheats on his wife (or vice versa) then can he be trusted not to cheat his employer? I tell you, I wouldn't want a person like that working for me. Let's be sure that we don't fall into the trap of taking God and His forgiveness for granted. I wonder, am I talking to someone today who is feeling thoroughly miserable because you have kept your distance from God and have tried to make it through on your own or put your confidence in your 'Assyrian' friends? I have a message from the Lord for you: this misery you feel can be 'productive' if you turn back to God and seek His face. God has allowed difficult times to come upon you, not in order to destroy you, but to prompt you toward repent-ance. Seek His face and, I promise you, the cloud of heaviness and misery will soon lift.

## Seeing Jesus in the Scriptures

The most critical words of Jesus were reserved not for those who society regarded as sinners, but for those who, though professing a faith in God, had hearts that were far from Him. Jesus ravaged and infuriated the religious Pharisees by exposing their hypocrisy and He even used a whip to cleanse the Temple of merchants and money changers (Matt. 15:7–9, 23:1–28, John 2:12–17).

WEEK FOUR

# Sins against God's love

## Opening Icebreaker

How should a professional football manager deal with his talented, well-paid son who plays for the team but who regularly misses training, overeats and ignores team strategies?

## Bible Reading

• Hosea 7:1–8:14

## Opening Our Eyes

Three more similes are put to work by Hosea to depict the spiritual condition of Ephraim – a half-baked cake, unnoticed grey hairs and a flustered dove. Take the first – a half-baked cake. A portion of life given to God and religious observances, but portions held back. Half-baked means 'halfway'. And no one can find peace in that. Peace can be found only in full commitment.

Look now at the second simile – unnoticed grey hairs. Is there anyone who has grey hair and hasn't yet noticed it? It sounds ridiculous, doesn't it! We are all well aware when our hair is turning grey; the mirror points it out to us. We are quick at picking up the signs of physical change or deterioration, but we are not so quick at spot-ting spiritual decline. Ephraim was like that – oblivious to the fact that they had crossed the line from faithfulness to adultery.

Hosea's third simile is that of a flustered dove. The whole nation of Israel had been released into the world to show the flight path to God, but instead she flitted around the Middle East looking for nesting places in Assyria and Egypt. The more Israel flapped, the less strength she had. This flighty bird would be netted and brought down.

We said earlier in our study that the problem with estrangement from God is not so much that it breaks His principles but that it breaks His heart. We sin not only against law but against love. Hear once again the pain in God's heart as He cries: 'They have strayed from me! ... they have rebelled against me! ... they speak lies against me ... they do not cry out to me.' The people wailed on their beds whenever God judged them (7:14) but they did not cry out in deep repentance or contrition. There is a great difference between 'wailing' and 'crying'. One is remorse, the other is repentance.

We get a glimpse, too, in 7:14 of the kind of praying these people engaged in. 'They gather together for grain and new wine but turn away from me.' They did not so much pray, '[Please] give us this day our daily bread' but 'Where's our daily bread?' Their petitions were filled more with 'demandingness' than devotion. The chapter ends in a rather bleak way with another of Hosea's powerful similes – 'they do not turn to the Most High; they are like a faulty bow.' Israel was God's strongbow, designed to aim the arrows of truth into the midst of the pagan nations. But now the bow was badly bent. God intended that Israel should convert the pagans, but instead the pagans had converted Israel. She worshipped where they worshipped and also in the same way that they worshipped. Hosea has one more indictment to make against Israel – that of misplaced trust. Oswald Chambers says that when you get to the very core of sin what you find is not just rebellion, but mistrust. Rebellion is there, he claims, but the root of it is mistrust. We are not sure that God can be trusted to give us what He says He will give – so we turn to other gods. We become self-sufficient and are no longer dependent on God.

How does God deal with His people when they are bent on going against Him? They must be judged. And remember it is not hatred that guides Him, but love. He loves His people too much to let them get away with things.

## Discussion Starters

1.  What is the difference between remorse and repentance?

    _____
    _____
    _____

2.  What is the difference between petitions and 'demandingness'?

    _____
    _____
    _____

3.  Why might the practice of prayer and worship offend God?

    _____
    _____
    _____

4.  How can our prayers and worship please God?

    _____
    _____
    _____

5.  How might believers be converted by unbelievers?

    _____
    _____
    _____

**6.** To what extent do you agree that the core of sin is not rebellion but misplaced trust?

_____

_____

_____

**7.** What is the role and goal of a true prophet of God?

_____

_____

_____

**8.** How can we ensure that we are quickly aware of and remedy any spiritual decline in our lives?

_____

_____

_____

**9.** Why was God's anger righteous and not vindictive?

_____

_____

_____

**10.** What similes would God use of the contemporary Church?

_____

_____

_____

## Personal Application

We are talking about ancient Israel, of course, but we could be talking about today's Church. How many half-baked Christians are there on the contemporary Christian scene? How many, I wonder, have crossed the line from honesty to dishonesty, purity to impurity and are not aware of it – unnoticed grey hair? And how many are like a flustered dove – they have turned away from the flight path to God? Time for a spiritual check-up. Hosea continues indicting Israel and his fourth accusation is this: 'For they have gone up to Assyria like a wild donkey wandering alone. Ephraim has sold herself to lovers... they have sold themselves among the nations' (8:9–10). The people of God tried to be diplomatic in courting the favour of other nations but their foreign policy was motivated more by gaining influential friendships than sharing with others the truths and principles which God had shared with them.

What a powerful lesson this provides for the contemporary Christian Church. We are not to ignore the world nor cut ourselves off from society, but we are to be careful in our contact with them. We need to approach the world with motives that are pure and not allow ourselves to become intrigued or entangled in its webs of duplicity and deceit. God put the Church in the world but we must watch that the devil doesn't put the world in the Church.

## Seeing Jesus in the Scriptures

Even though He was the Son of God, Jesus remained totally dependent on His Father. He could only work and speak as God showed Him (John 5:19; 8:28–29).

WEEK FIVE

# An adulterous love

## Opening Icebreaker

What may cause a marriage partner to commit adultery?

## Bible Reading

* Hosea 9:1–10:15

## Opening Our Eyes

This section give us a glimpse of the delight that was in God's heart during the days of His early relationship with His bride, Israel. 'When I found Israel, it was like finding grapes in the desert … like seeing the early fruit on the fig-tree' (9:10). There can be nothing more beautiful or enjoyable in life than the early days of marriage when physical and emotional closeness bring such sweetness to the soul. How sad it is when such sweetness turns sour.

One of the first turning points in Israel's relationship with God came at Shittim when the Israelite men indulged in sexual immorality with the Moabite women and worship-ped their gods (Num. 25). Hosea tells us that when they did this they became 'as vile as the thing they loved' (9:10). Israel's surrender to both physical and spiritual adultery will have consequences. The first thing to go will be Israel's 'glory' – the glory of God's presence. But worse is to come – the family tree of the northern tribes (Ephraim) will be lopped off and there will be barrenness and infertility. Don't feel sympathetic towards Israel. She is going to get what she deserved. This is tough stuff, but God is going to see the matter through to the bitter end. Israel must take God's cure or take the consequences. The phrases: 'Sow for yourselves righteousness… break up your unploughed ground' have been used on count-less occasions down the years by preachers calling the Church back to repentance; and particularly the phrase, 'it is time to seek the LORD' (Hosea 10:12). In other words, 'there is very little time left'.

One of the most hallowed spots in Israel was Gilgal. It was the place where Joshua set up 12 stones to celebrate the successful crossing of the Jordan and thus became Israel's first place of worship in the promised land. What exactly happened at Gilgal that caused God to say, 'I hated them there' is something about

which we cannot be certain. It is likely that it had something
to do with the false worship and prostitution that flourished
at certain shrines – an issue we dealt with when looking at
Hosea 4:14–19.

I have made this point before but I want to make it again:
whenever we read about God hating His people we have got to
see that divine hatred is quite different from the kind of hate
we may find arising in our own hearts when we are let down
by a loved one. It's surprising how quickly love can sour in
a person who has been rejected by a spouse. Time and time
again I have heard a man or woman say about an unfaithful
partner: 'I have no love left. I'm afraid my love has turned to
hate.' This is because often human love is not strong enough
to bear the hurt of wounded love and calls on other emotions
to sustain it. Hatred, for example, is a much more acceptable
feeling than unassuaged hurt.

But the divine heart is different. God hates in a different way
from us, with no pique and no animosity. He hates the sin
but loves the sinner. And the expression of His hatred is not
to make Himself feel better but for His people's good. Arising
from the divine hatred or what we described earlier as 'tough
love', Israel will be driven out of her home and the people will
become 'wanderers among the nations'. But all the time, *all*
the time, God has reconciliation in view.

**Discussion Starters**

1. What would be examples of spiritual adultery?

2. Does the concept of God feeling hate disturb you?

3. How is God's hate expressed?

4. Why does God discipline us? (See Hebrews 12:4–11.)

5. How does discipline differ from punishment?

**6.** How can we be in the world but not of the world?
(See John 17:13–19.)

_____

_____

_____

**7.** Why is loving the world compared to adultery and
hating God?

_____

_____

_____

**8.** How can we appreciate the blessings of God's world
without it becoming idolatry?

_____

_____

_____

**9.** How might we reject God by depending on our
own strength?

_____

_____

_____

**10.** Is it wrong for a Christian to be wealthy?

_____

_____

_____

## Personal Application

God will not allow His people to get away with adulterous behaviour, whether it be ancient Israel or the modern-day Church. The apostle James uses a startling expression when he says that any Christian who flirts with the world is an 'adulterer' (James 4:4). An adulterer? Surely not. A fool perhaps. Or shallow. But an adulterer? Yes, an adulterer – someone who gives him or herself in a close relationship with someone other than his or her spouse. But James goes even further. 'Friendship with the world,' he says, 'is hatred towards God.' Adulterer! Hatred towards God! These are shocking words. But then that is what worldly-minded believers need. They need to be shocked. A similar thought is expressed in 1 John 2:15–17 where we are warned not 'to love the world'. Remember the verse from the parable of the sower which says, 'The seed that fell among thorns stands for those who hear, but as they go on their way they are choked by life's worries, riches and pleasures, and they do not mature' (Luke 8:14). Paul explained to Timothy that, 'the love of money is a root of all kinds of evil. Some people, eager for money, have wandered from the faith and pierced themselves with many griefs' (1 Tim. 6:10).

## Seeing Jesus in the Scriptures

Jesus rejected the world's riches and methods when He was tempted in the wilderness (Matt. 4.1–11). Although He lived in the world and enjoyed its food, clothing and home comforts, Jesus did not allow these things to capture His heart and lure Him away from His fellowship with the Father.

WEEK SIX

# The agony of God's love

## Opening Icebreaker

Describe an occasion when you lost something that was
precious to you and how you felt.

## Bible Reading

- Hosea 11:1–12:14

## Opening Our Eyes

Chapter 11 'exposes us to the mind and heart of God in human terms.' God now describes Himself not as a bridegroom yearning over His adulterous wife, or a farmer tending his grapes, but as a parent grieving over a rebellious child. Some Christians have difficulty with the figure of God as Father because their own experience of an earthly father has been negative, and thus they form a negative image of fatherhood and tend to project that selfsame image on to God. But we must remember that when the Bible depicts God as Father it is talking about Him in terms of the best that is in human fatherhood, not the worst. Listen to these words and sense the nostalgia

in them: 'When Israel was a child, I loved him... But the more I called Israel, the further they went from me' (11:1–2). It continues: 'It was I who taught Ephraim to walk, taking them by the arms; but they did not realise it was I who healed them.' Every parent reading these descriptive lines will easily identify with them. Can you not remember coaxing your children to take their first steps, picking them up when they stumbled, kissing the hurt away when they were in pain? How wonderful were those moments! But children grow up and some, when they get into adolescence, turn away from parental love and forget what they owe to their early relationships. How does a parent feel when that happens? Saddened and deeply hurt. God feels the same way too. Divine love is more, not less, vulnerable and ardent than ours.

How could anyone turn away from such a love as this? That is what Israel did, however, but God is committed to His people and, no matter what, He will not give them up. If they will not return to God, then they will have to return to Egypt and experience the yoke of a hard taskmaster (Hosea 11:5).

But note how the pronouncement of judgment is interrupted with the cry: 'How can I give you up, Ephraim? How can I hand you over, Israel? ... My heart is changed within me; all my compassion is aroused' (11:8). The very thought of forsaking His people and abandoning them to their plight arouses deep feelings in the heart of the Almighty. His big heart is caught up in a tremendous tug-of-war. Justice pulls in one direction and mercy in the other. Should Israel be destroyed like the cities God had flattened long ago – Admah and Zeboiim (Gen. 14:8) – or should she be spared? Perhaps nowhere else in the whole of Scripture do we see the fierce emotion that burns in the heart of God for His people. Does God have emotion? Let the question never come up again. The Almighty anguishes over His people's infidelities, grieves over their wandering affections and cries out in pain when His marriage shows signs of breaking down.

Chapter 12 ends by making a point concerning prophecy which a cursory reading may not pick up. 'The LORD used a prophet to bring Israel up from Egypt, by a prophet he cared for him' (v13). Some in Israel may have thought of Moses as a great leader but the Almighty makes clear here that his main ministry was not to stand before Pharaoh but to stand before God. He was a prophet first and a leader second. Thus the spiritual nature of leadership and specifically the Exodus (not merely a liberation movement) is underlined.

## Discussion Starters

1.  How might your experiences of earthly parents shape your perceptions of your heavenly Father?

    _____

    _____

    _____

2.  How does God expose Himself to us in human terms?

    _____

    _____

    _____

3.  What emotions does Scripture reveal God to have?

    _____

    _____

    _____

4.  What arouses God's compassion?

    _____

    _____

    _____

5.  What arouses God's anger?

    _____

    _____

    _____

**6.** Why is God vulnerable to pain and what hurts Him?

_____

_____

_____

**7.** How does God reconcile judgment and mercy?

_____

_____

_____

**8.** What are the main requirements for leadership?

_____

_____

_____

**9.** What emotions did Jesus experience in Matthew 23:37?

_____

_____

_____

**10.** How should we deal with pain in our own lives?

_____

_____

_____

## Personal Application

Hosea zooms in on Ephraim's double-talk and double-dealing – 'Ephraim feeds on the wind' – and he warns that such deceit has not gone unnoticed by God. Double-talk, double-dealing and lies always end in disaster, wherever they are practised. A politician in Britain said recently, 'A certain amount of double-talk is necessary if you are to get on in politics'; but Gladstone, a nineteenth-century prime minister of Britain said, 'Nothing that is morally wrong can be politically right.' The laws that govern right and wrong are of universal application. Malcolm Muggeridge put it best when he said, 'Truth and honesty have their source in the bosom of God and their voices when heard bring harmony to the world.' The average Israelite had lived so long with duplicity and deceit that his spiritual compass was no longer functioning correctly. What's wrong with cheating on a tax return or taking a few odds and ends from work that nobody will miss? This is God's paraphrased answer: 'Is this what I redeemed you, brought you out of Egypt for – that you be no better than the Canaanites? If that's the case then you had better go back to living in tents!' How sad it is when Christians live no better than the people of the world they have been redeemed from. Let us be people of truth and honesty.

## Seeing Jesus in the Scriptures

In Matthew 23:37 we see the depth of love and compassion that existed in the heart of Jesus for a rebellious people. He could not stand idly by, but that love caused Him to act and to act sacrificially.

WEEK SEVEN

# God's love wins – a happy ending

## Opening Icebreaker

What parts of a marriage ceremony do you think are most significant and enjoyable?

## Bible Reading

- Hosea 13:1–14:9

## Opening Our Eyes

As we draw near to the end of Hosea's prophecy, he sums up the root cause of Israel's spiritual apostasy in this way: the nation 'became guilty of Baal worship and died' (13:1). The people of Israel had turned from depending on the Lord to depending on another god. The Almighty could roll back the waters of the Red Sea, provide for them in the wilderness, and bring them into the promised land, but was He big enough to support them after they had settled down in their new environment? Israel was not sure. Perhaps a change of lifestyle demanded a change of god? Baal proved an attractive competitor; after all, had he not kept the land of Canaan green and fertile? It was not long before the Israelites transferred their allegiance to him and when they did, they 'died' as surely as Adam and Eve died when they partook of the forbidden fruit in the Garden of Eden.

Can there to be a happy ending for Israel? Yes, there can. Following repentance, her life will not just be a bed of roses but of blossoming flowers! 'I will heal their waywardness and love them freely... be like the dew to Israel; he will blossom like a lily' (14:4–5). Israel had discarded God a long time ago and thus is as dry and arid as a desert, but one day God will come raining down on the Israelites so that the nation will become like a cedar of Lebanon (v5b). The roots of the cedars of Lebanon, I am told, sink deep into the earth and they are almost as long as the tree is tall. It is almost impossible to dig up a Lebanon cedar, say the experts; you have to blast it with dynamite, so firmly rooted is it in the ground.

But there's more. Israel's 'splendour will be like an olive tree, his fragrance like a cedar of Lebanon' (14:6). Israel will no longer have the cheap smell of a prostitute but have about her the perfume of God. She will also be as fruitful in her love as the fruitful vineyards are with grapes. When is all this to take place? In the future.

I have mentioned before the great significance of Israel having been restored to the land in our own day and generation, and although her troubles are still many, the day will come (is perhaps not all that distant) when her eyes will be opened to see that God has already sent the true Messiah. What a day that will be, when the veil over Israel's eyes will be removed and she will see for herself that the Messiah she rejected is none other than the second person of the Trinity. Another prophet speaking of that great future occasion put it thus: 'They will look on me, the one they have pierced' (Zech. 12:10).

Isaiah chapter 62 also uses the picture of a desolate woman restored to a fulfilling marriage: 'for the LORD will take delight in you, and your land will be married... as a bridegroom rejoices over his bride, so will your God rejoice over you' (Isa. 62:4–5). Although there may be dark and confusing times ahead, God's love will win and there will be a happy ending with God and His people enjoying their covenant love relationship for all eternity.

## Discussion Starters

**1.** Why did God choose the picture of a marriage relationship in Hosea to convey spiritual truth?

**2.** What is the problem with being fully satisfied with life?

**3.** What is the central message of Hosea?

**4.** Which characteristics of God are revealed in the book of Hosea?

**5.** Describe how God feels about people who do not worship Him.

**6.** How have your own concepts of God been deepened or changed in studying Hosea?

_____

_____

_____

**7.** How can we ensure that our own relationship with God is pure?

_____

_____

_____

**8.** How should we relate to those who reject God?

_____

_____

_____

**9.** Which parts of our study have you found most difficult or challenging?

_____

_____

_____

**10.** How do we see and understand more about Jesus through Hosea?

_____

_____

_____

## Personal Application

We are called to reflect the sacrificial love of God to others
through our own relationships, even to those who have
hurt or betrayed us. When we love like that, people will
know we are truly Christ's disciples (John 13:34–35). When
God's command came, Hosea appeared not to hesitate. No
quibbling, no prevarication. God spoke, and Hosea acted.
He was, as one commentator puts it, 'God's action man'.
Hosea knew the first rule of loving God is – obedience.
Archbishop William Temple, said, 'Every revelation of God
is a demand, and the way to knowledge of God is obedience.'
Our relationship with God rises and falls at the point of
obedience. When we stop obeying, God stops revealing. And
always remember – whenever God's finger points the way to
anything, His hand always provides the power. It is ours to be
willing; it is His to be supporting.

The closing words must be directed to those of us who form
not part of God's bride – Israel – but of Christ's bride – the
Church. What is our relationship like with Him? Do we give
Him cause to grieve over our way-wardness, our flirting with
other gods? If you take all that Hosea has said and apply it to
your own relationship with Christ, then it will be pleasure
and not pain that will fill your Saviour's heart.

## Seeing Jesus in the Scriptures

Jesus unhesitatingly obeyed the Father's command to
renounce the glory of heaven for a gory and a sin-stained
humanity. He became the friend of sinners, who in turn will
become His glorious bride for all eternity.

# Leader's Notes

## Week One: A love that will not let go

### Opening Icebreaker

The icebreaker is designed to encourage us to think about the feelings of disappointment that arise when love is frustrated and particularly when the object of our love not only spurns our affections but almost deliberately sets out to betray and hurt us. It is only when we begin to understand God's feelings of disappointment and unrequited love that we can understand the message of Hosea. God does not reject the one who has rejected Him, but instead He seeks to show His errant lover the folly of her ways and woo her back to Himself.

### Bible Readings

Each session deals with two chapters of Hosea. Depending on the time available you might decide to only read a few appropriate verses. If you do read all of both chapters you could split them into sections and discuss them one at a time.

### Aim of the Session

Long ago in the wilderness God had made a vow to His bride when He promised to cherish her and keep her, and in exchange the bride had promised to obey. The honeymoon was a protracted one and spent in a wilderness but eventually God carried His bride over the threshold of the River Jordan and into the promised land. The Almighty had promised her a home – and here it was.

But no sooner was the bride set down in her new home than she began associating with the local gods, particularly Baal. The god Baal was known as the god of fertility and many of the Israelites were beguiled by his apparent prowess in producing the good things of life – food, wine, water and so

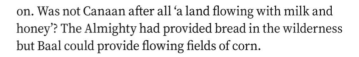

on. Was not Canaan after all 'a land flowing with milk and honey'? The Almighty had provided bread in the wilderness but Baal could provide flowing fields of corn.

The question arises: had the situation which developed between God and His bride Israel happened also to Hosea and Gomer? Undoubtedly, yes. Confronted by her husband over her flirtatious and adulterous ways (2:2) Gomer said to herself: 'I will go after my lovers, who give me my food and my water, my wool and my linen, my oil and my drink' (2:5).

There is only one way some people will learn a lesson: the hard way, through trouble. Gomer and Israel were to fall on difficult times. This would be the only way they would turn back to their husbands and cry for help. The statement, 'I am now going to allure her; I will lead her into the desert and speak tenderly to her' (2:14) is one that ought to be emblazoned on every one of our hearts. If we do not hear His word and heed it in trouble-free times, then God will see to it that we are drawn into troublesome times. We sometimes have to be put on our backs before we look up into His face.

Is God too harsh with us when He allures us into the desert? Not at all. The divine lover does it because sometimes that is the only way He can get our attention. Notice that when He gets us there He speaks tenderly to us. No thundering sermons on 'Why did you do this?' or 'Why did you do that?' Rather, a gentle entreating that goes something like this: 'Can't you see that you are not only hurting me but hurting yourself by the way you have been living? Will you not stop and consider that the way I plan for you to live is the way that is best for you? My way is not alien to your personality. You were made for happiness but true happiness can only be found in me.'

# **Week Two:** A love that is out of this world

### **Opening Icebreaker**

Some examples could be a parent giving one of their own kidneys to their child, animals protecting their young from fierce predators or servicemen dying in defence of their comrades in wartime. Contrast these examples with Romans 5:7–8.

### **Bible Readings**

As well as verses from Hosea try to read Romans 5:7–8 as above which is quoted in full in the section of the notes entitled Seeing Jesus in the Scriptures.

### **Aim of the Session**

Like Gomer, Israel was hooked on the physical side of life, and thought of love only in terms of sensual feelings. Israel and Gomer were two of a kind – they wanted love without having to give love. They focused on getting rather than giving. But there is to come a time of reckoning. Both brides have to find out what love and marriage is all about. Once again, however, we note that God's last word is not judgment. After a time of pruning and discipline, the people of Israel will once again turn to the Lord their God, says Hosea. 'They will come trembling to the LORD and to his blessings in the last days' (Hosea 3:5). What are these 'blessings' about which the prophet speaks? Look back to Hosea 2:18–23 and you will see. 'I will make a covenant for them with the beasts of the field... I will betroth you to me for ever... I will show my love' and so on. When God made His marriage vow to Israel at the foot of Sinai, He was not pretending. He promised her paradise and one day paradise is what she is going to get. What happens to Gomer from here on? We don't know. Nothing more is said about her. But there is one thing about which we can be certain – she was in good hands.

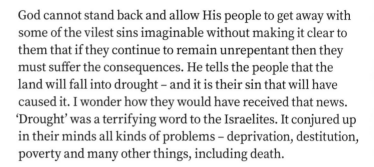

God cannot stand back and allow His people to get away with some of the vilest sins imaginable without making it clear to them that if they continue to remain unrepentant then they must suffer the consequences. He tells the people that the land will fall into drought – and it is their sin that will have caused it. I wonder how they would have received that news. 'Drought' was a terrifying word to the Israelites. It conjured up in their minds all kinds of problems – deprivation, destitution, poverty and many other things, including death.

What in effect the Almighty was saying was this: 'Now look here. You have been guilty of wandering affections and have run out on me, your husband, more than once. You have gone to your paramour, Baal, and given him your appreciation for providing you with food and drink when it was me all the time who was your provider. I am the breadwinner in this family and I have never failed you. Now because of your stubborn refusal to acknowledge my provision for you and my constant care, I will show you where your real resources lie. I will not provide any rain for your crops any more. Then we will see whether Baal will help you. Be warned – it's going to be a long, hot summer.'

How can such a people regain their spiritual understanding? It is not enough to feel remorse or regret. There is only one way – repentance. True repentance involves a change of behaviour whereas remorse alone is a feeling of sorrow that can result in self-pity or guilt without a transformation of lifestyle. (See 2 Corinthians 7:8–11). How sad that the people of God have to be chastened into submission instead of continually resting there.

# Week Three: An unrequited love

## Opening Icebreaker

The pursuit of ambitions, possessions, pleasures and relationships instead of God and His kingdom shows us that Hosea's prophecy is also applicable in today's world.

## Bible Readings

It could be helpful to refer to Romans 1:18–32 in addition to the main reference from Hosea.

## Aim of the Session

In this section Israel is accused of two things: habitual sin and lack of understanding of God. 'Their deeds do not permit them to return,' says Hosea (5:4). The more deeply one sins and the more one continues in that sin, the harder it is to repent. Idolatry had taken a firm grip on Israel and they were in a kind of spiritual stranglehold – victims of their own foolishness.

Hosea knows himself to be God's ambassador to Israel, and that he has a message to both the people and the priests. Now he includes those who were members of Israel's royal family. More will be said about the royal court in chapter 7 but for now all three sections of the realm – people, priests and the royals – come under fire. The entire nation is corrupt. Mizpah and Tabor were associated with significant spiritual events – Mizpah with Samuel and Saul (1 Sam. 7:5–16; 10:17–25), and Tabor with the victory of Deborah over Barak in Judges 4. Now, however, these places were infamous because of the way in which altars or shrines to other gods were littering the areas. 'Anyone with deep spiritual intent moving into these places could easily become trapped,' says Hosea. 'You have been a snare at Mizpah, a net spread out on Tabor.'

wonder what Hosea would say, were he alive today and saw he spiritual apostasy in some of our churches and theological training institutions. Many a young minister entering a seminary nowadays goes in with faith and confidence in the gospel and comes out with uncertainty and doubt. This doesn't happen to everyone, of course, and there are an abundance of Bible-believing institutions, but increasingly in my travels I meet many young ministers who tell me how their faith lies torn and bleeding because a theological course they have taken has systematically dismantled their confidence in the Scriptures. There are equivalents to Mizpah and Tabor in our contemporary Christian society. God would not leave Israel without a day of reckoning, and a day of reckoning will come for these modern counterparts as well. Let us ensure that the places of spiritual victories in the past do not become places of spiritual idolatry in the present.

Hosea 6:1–3 might suggest that Hosea is leading the people in a prayer of repentance but most commentators view it as Israel's own words used in a facile and insincere way. The sentiment being expressed here by Israel, says Derek Kidner, is similar to the famous but presumptuous words of Catherine the Great: 'The good Lord will pardon, that's his trade.' God is exposing, for all to see, the light-hearted approach of Israel towards their spiritual condition. Psalm 78:34–36 explains; 'Whenever God slew them, they would seek him… But then they would flatter him with their mouths, lying to him with their tongues.' The people of God, covenant people remember, seemed to have no idea of what faithful love was all about. They made light of their own spiritual state and of the agony that God felt over their unrequited love. It is a broken marriage that God is concerned about here, not just a little tiff between friends. Why God puts up with an erring people is a mystery. But how glad we ought to be that He does.

# Week Four: Sins against God's love

## Opening Icebreaker

This is another exercise designed to help us understand the
emotions and actions of God in dealing with His beloved but
wayward Israel.

## Bible Readings

These chapters deal with Israel's arrogant refusal to truly
repent, and wilful idolatry

## Aim of the Session

'The role of a prophet is to surprise, disrupt, and open the door
to hope,' says American writer, Dan Allender. He continues,
'A prophet speaks truth in a way that gets the attention of the
listener and sneaks into the issues of the soul through an
unexpected crack in the heart.' This approach does not always
guarantee a response, of course, but the true prophet works
like a saboteur, using words and drama and everything at his
disposal to undermine self-centredness and self-interest.

In this section, Hosea uses once again a collection of brilliant
similes to expose the corruption going on in almost every
section of the nation's life. He focuses on the palace and
accuses Israel's royal family of doing nothing to stem the
tide of evil. His vivid word-picture of an oven that needs no
stoking once the bread has begun to rise is suggestive of the
'self-propagating passion' resident in their hearts.

It is important to realise that Hosea, being a true prophet, was
concerned not only with exposure but also with restoration. A
preacher or teacher who delights in announcing judgment but
has no heart for restoration is not following the biblical pattern.
Hosea's own love had been fashioned by the circumstances
in which God had placed him, and he understood more than
anyone how God felt towards His rebellious bride.

e one thing that emerges most clearly from Hosea's lictment of God's bride is her arrogant self-sufficiency. e opposite of self-sufficiency is dependency, but clearly the pple of Israel are no longer dependent on God. They rely re on the surrounding nations than they do on their creator. od's patience has reached its limit and now judgment is not ar from being poured out. How did the people react to the warnings given them by God? Typically they said, 'O God, we acknowledge you!' The bride claimed to acknowledge her husband but God knew better. Hosea piles up the evidence.

First, the people rejected 'good'. Second, they chose their own kings (Hosea 8:4). Third, they created their own gods (vv4–6). The people collected together their silver and gold and went into the god-manufacturing business. First off the production line was a golden calf. Memories of Sinai here? The last word, however, is always with God. How important it is to remember this. They will make a golden calf; God will break it. Our choices are not the final thing. There is one whose choices supersede ours.

Someone has said that spiritual maturity can be measured by where we put our trust. Is it in God or in things? In the Saviour or in silver? In God or in gold? There is nothing wrong, of course, in wealth or in having a healthy bank account. I wish mine was healthier than it is; but that is not where we put our trust. Our trust must be in the Lord. He can soon blow on wealth and it will end up, as Haggai said, like putting coins in a bag full of holes (Haggai 1:6).

There is an old saying that 'one has to be cruel to be kind'. What we are seeing in God's pronouncements of judgment on Israel is not spite or spleen, but righteous anger. Righteous anger is anger directed toward the good of others, not just spite or spleen at what is happening to oneself. God's judgments on His people are not retributive, but remedial.

# Week Five: An adulterous love

## Opening Icebreaker

We need to be sensitive to those who may have been involved in adultery whether willing agent or innocent victim. Remember that many people eventually come to regret adulterous relationships – 'the grass looks greener on the other side of the fence' but it is actually bitter and may cause considerable pain.

## Bible Readings

Additional references are given in other sections and may be helpful if time permits.

## Aim of the Session

Some may regard the continued admonitions which Hosea gives to Israel as somewhat tedious and repetitive. Why all this detail, all these specifics? God gives His people clear information on what will happen if they disobey, so that no one can say, 'I didn't realise the consequences.' No greater measurement of guilt could be accorded to the people of Israel than to compare them with Gibeah (9:9). The depth of depravity to which the people of Gibeah descended is comparable to that of Sodom and Gomorrah, including the act of sodomy (see Judges 20–21 and also Genesis 18–19).

In Hosea 10:1 God speaks of Israel as a spreading (or luxuriant) vine. Here again we can feel the anguish in the divine heart as He thinks back to the early days of His marriage to Israel. Previously (9:10) God had described the pleasure He experienced in His relationship with Israel as like 'grapes in the desert', but now the image is extended to that of a spreading, sprawling vine, bringing forth bitter fruit (see Deut. 32:32). A people so full of promise have become a disappointment. The more they prospered physically the more they declined spiritually. They decorated altars and

built more, attempting to accommodate the many cults which flourished in Canaan. They pretended to worship the Lord at these altars but their worship was false – and an attempt to unify that which cannot be unified. In Hosea 10:10 God refers once again to the sin of Gibeah and reprimands Israel for their 'double sin'. Jeremiah refers to 'two evils' (Jer. 2:13) – forsaking the Lord and turning to idols. It is bad enough to turn from God, but to turn to idols is reprehensible. God's judgment on the shrines that had been used for a dual purpose – the worship of God and the worship of Baal – is that they will be covered with thorns and thistles. The only other occasion where thorns and thistles are paired in this way is in Genesis 3:18 where they are referred to as part of the curse which followed Adam and Eve's disobedience. Israel's fall, just like Adam and Eve's, is to be met by the growth of thorns and thistles that will prevent the shrines being used – a symbol of divine displeasure. In Samuel's day, Israel's tears had been for the captured ark of the covenant, but now the people will shed tears over a captured idol – the calf-idol erected at Beth Aven (10:5). Can anything be more sad than seeing the glory of God exchanged for an idol? And people weeping over it when it is carried away!

There is one final phrase that leads us to the heart of Israel's great problems – 'you have depended on your own strength' (10:13). I have worked with people all my life to try and find the genesis of spiritual problems and there is no doubt in my mind as to what it is: self-dependency rather than God-dependency. This is what throws us into one difficulty after another – we are drawn to relying more on our own resources than on God's. People ask: 'Are we close to revival?' 'Not yet,' I reply. We are not weak enough. Before we can become strong we must become weak. Weak in our own strength; strong in His.

# **Week Six:** The agony of God's love

### **Opening Icebreaker**
God has not just lost something, He has lost His most
treasured possession – 'the apple of His eye' (Deut. 32:10).

### **Bible Readings**
Read also Matthew 23:37 to see the agony of Jesus for
the people.

### **Aim of the Session**
We realise that God was caught up in a tremendous tug-of-war.
Justice pulled His heart strings one way, and love and mercy
pulled equally hard in the other direction. Now we see how
God has decided: 'I will not carry out my fierce anger, nor will
I devastate Ephraim' (11:9). This must not be taken to mean
that God had changed His mind about disciplining the people;
what it meant was that He would not destroy them or cast
them away. The people of God would find themselves in the
furnace of affliction but they would survive and have a future.

If God's heart had been human, then Israel would not have
survived. Such a rebellious child would have been left to their
own devices. But God is different. 'I am God and not a man –
the Holy One among you' (v9). That means He is completely
separate from us and our ways. Human love is prone to give
up when the object of its love is rebellious and unresponsive.
But God's love is persistent, unquenchable, everlasting. God
will not discipline His child in anger but will discipline in love.
Exile will bring the people to their senses. What is Ephraim's
response to the divine plea that the people should return to
their God? Regrettably it is one of brazenness and arrogance.
The Amplified Version translates Hosea 12:7–8: 'Canaan, [Israel
– whose ideals have sunk to those of Canaan] is a trader; the
balances of deceit are in his hand; he loves to oppress and
defraud. Ephraim has said, Ah, but I have become rich; I have

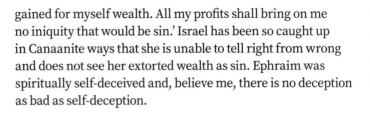

gained for myself wealth. All my profits shall bring on me no iniquity that would be sin.' Israel has been so caught up in Canaanite ways that she is unable to tell right from wrong and does not see her extorted wealth as sin. Ephraim was spiritually self-deceived and, believe me, there is no deception as bad as self-deception.

Chapter 11 closes with words of promise: 'he will roar like a lion... They will come from Egypt trembling like sparrows... I will settle them in their homes.' The lion-hearted God will call His people home. Whatever stage of history God had in mind here, it is worth noting that in our own generation Israel has 'come home'. Troubles still assail her, however, and always will, until the day comes in the future when through a radical and national repentance she will enter into a deep, intimate relationship with God once again.

What's Hosea's point in telling the story of Jacob in chapter 12? It is made clear in verse 6: 'you must return to your God; maintain love and justice, and wait for your God always.' Israel had been called by God to strive with Him for the hearts of the pagan nations but the only thing the people strove for was themselves. Instead of Jacob becoming Israel, Israel had become Jacob – a nation of grabbers. The only way this can be changed, says Hosea, is by a 'return to your God' (v6). But note the words carefully: 'you *must* return to your God.' Just as Jacob was born selfish and had to meet with God before he could be changed, so the nation of Israel must come the same way and strive with God for His blessing. Israel's nature could not be changed apart from an encounter with God. Neither can yours or mine.

## Week Seven: God's love wins - a happy ending

### Opening Icebreaker
As we conclude the book of Hosea we begin to think about our
eternal relationship as part of the bride of Christ, including
the great marriage supper of the lamb.

### Bible Readings
It may also be helpful to refer to scriptures that speak
of the marriage relationship of Christ and His Church
(eg Eph. 5:23–32; 2 Cor. 11:2; Rev. 19:6–9, 21:1–4).

### Aim of the Session
How appropriate that among the last words of Hosea's
prophecy we observe God's great heart of love lamenting
the fact that even though His bride will one day return, she
has persistently spurned Him. God is heard crying like a
demented husband whose wife has left him for another man.
'O Ephraim, what more have I to do with idols?' (14:8). Can God
be compared to idols? It is unthinkable. Can the strength and
might of Egypt or Assyria be compared to the strength of the
everlasting God? Do they care as He cares? Ephraim, whose
name means 'God made me fruitful', will only live up to his
name when he comes back to God.

Hosea's work is nearly done. He has put the case on God's
behalf. But now comes a postscript. The Amplified Bible puts
it best: 'Who is wise, that he may understand these things?
Prudent, that he may know them? For the ways of the Lord are
right, and the [uncompromisingly] just shall walk in them; but
transgressors shall stumble and fall in them' (v9). If I were to
paraphrase Hosea's postscript it would sound something like
this: 'If you have any sense at all, you will get the message. If you
have any semblance of wisdom, you will take the point. And
what is the point? This: those who walk with God walk safely;
those who won't, have to stumble tragically on their own.'

One liberally minded theologian describes God's threats in Hosea as 'petty jealousy'. Well, it is jealousy all right, but not 'petty' jealousy. Divine jealousy must not be confused with human jealousy. Human jealousy is usually full of self-interest – this should not be happening to me. Divine jealousy is characterised by other-interest – this should not be happening to you. In God, jealousy is a fiery concern that others will attempt to give His people what He knows only He can give. When I first read the words of Hosea as a young student of the Scriptures, I recoiled in horror and said to myself, 'I don't want to serve a God who treats people like that, no matter what they have done.' I hesitated to enter the Christian ministry – all because of these words. I shared my concern with my godly pastor, who helped me understand that a God who so clearly is love (the cross demonstrates that) must have a good reason to allow such things to happen, and that I should interpret the strange and mysterious actions of God by what I know about Him through the cross, not the other way round. That is the way I now approach all the difficulties presented to me by life, or the Scriptures. I know God is love and, though I find it difficult to reconcile some of His judgments with the concept of His love, I believe that ultimately everything God does will be fully and perfectly justified. Therefore I take my stand with that of another who said, 'Will not the Judge of all the earth do right?' (Gen. 18:25).

The book of Revelation confirms that God's love will win and there will be a happy ending where Christ and His bride will enjoy their union in everlasting love.

# Notes...

# Notes...

# The *Cover to Cover* Bible Study Series

**1 Corinthians**
*Growing a Spirit-filled church*
ISBN: 978-1-85345-374-8

**2 Corinthians**
*Restoring harmony*
ISBN: 978-1-85345-551-3

**1,2,3 John**
*Walking in the truth*
ISBN: 978-1-78259-763-6

**1 Peter**
*Good reasons for hope*
ISBN: 978-1-78259-088-0

**2 Peter**
*Living in the light of God's
promises*
ISBN: 978-1-78259-403-1

**23rd Psalm**
*The Lord is my shepherd*
ISBN: 978-1-85345-449-3

**1 Timothy**
*Healthy churches – effective
Christians*
ISBN: 978-1-85345-291-8

**2 Timothy and Titus**
*Vital Christianity*
ISBN: 978-1-85345-338-0

**Abraham**
*Adventures of faith*
ISBN: 978-1-78259-089-7

**Acts 1-12**
*Church on the move*
ISBN: 978-1-85345-574-2

**Acts 13-28**
*To the ends of the earth*
ISBN: 978-1-85345-592-6

**Barnabas**
*Son of encouragement*
ISBN: 978-1-85345-911-5

**Bible Genres**
*Hearing what the Bible really says*
ISBN: 978-1-85345-987-0

**Daniel**
*Living boldly for God*
ISBN: 978-1-85345-986-3

**David**
*A man after God's own heart*
ISBN: 978-1-78259-444-4

**Ecclesiastes**
*Hard questions and spiritual
answers*
ISBN: 978-1-85345-371-7

**Elijah**
*A man and his God*
ISBN: 978-1-85345-575-9

**Elisha**
*A lesson in faithfulness*
ISBN: 978-1-78259-494-9

**Ephesians**
*Claiming your inheritance*
ISBN: 978-1-85345-229-1

**Esther**
*For such a time as this*
ISBN: 978-1-85345-511-7

**Ezekiel**
*A prophet for all times*
ISBN: 978-1-78259-836-7

**Fruit of the Spirit**
*Growing more like Jesus*
ISBN: 978-1-85345-375-5

**Galatians**
*Freedom in Christ*
ISBN: 978-1-85345-648-0

**Genesis 1-11**
*Foundations of reality*
ISBN: 978-1-85345-404-2

**Genesis 12-50**
*Founding fathers of faith*
ISBN: 978-1-78259-960-9

**God's Rescue Plan**
*Finding God's fingerprints on
human history*
ISBN: 978-1-85345-294-9

**Great Prayers of the Bible**
*Applying them to our lives tod*
ISBN: 978-1-85345-253-6

**Habakkuk**
*Choosing God's way*
ISBN: 978-1-78259-843-5

**Haggai**
*Motivating God's people*
ISBN: 978-1-78259-686-8

**Hebrews**
*Jesus – simply the best*
ISBN: 978-1-85345-337-3

**Isaiah 1-39**
*Prophet to the nations*
ISBN: 978-1-85345-510-0

**Isaiah 40-66**
*Prophet of restoration*
ISBN: 978-1-85345-550-6

**Jacob**
*Taking hold of God's blessing*
ISBN: 978-1-78259-685-1

**James**
*Faith in action*
ISBN: 978-1-85345-293-2

**Jeremiah**
*The passionate prophet*
ISBN: 978-1-85345-372-4

**Job**
*The source of wisdom*
ISBN: 978-1-78259-992-0

**Joel**
*Getting real with God*
ISBN: 978-1-78951-927-2

**John's Gospel**
*Exploring the seven miraculous signs*
ISBN: 978-1-85345-295-6

**Jonah**
*Rescued from the depths*
ISBN: 978-1-78259-762-9

**Joseph**
*The power of forgiveness and reconciliation*
ISBN: 978-1-85345-252-9

**Joshua 1-10**
*Hand in hand with God*
ISBN: 978-1-85345-542-7

**Joshua 11-24**
*Called to service*
ISBN: 978-1-78951-138-3

**Judges 1-8**
*The spiral of faith*
ISBN: 978-1-85345-681-7

**Judges 9-21**
*Learning to live God's way*
ISBN: 978-1-85345-910-8

**Luke**
*A prescription for living*
ISBN: 978-1-78259-270-9

**Mark**
*Life as it is meant to be lived*
ISBN: 978-1-85345-233-8

**Mary**
*The mother of Jesus*
ISBN: 978-1-78259-402-4

**Moses**
*Face to face with God*
ISBN: 978-1-85345-336-6

**Names of God**
*Exploring the depths of God's character*
ISBN: 978-1-85345-680-0

**Nehemiah**
*Principles for life*
ISBN: 978-1-85345-335-9

**Parables**
*Communicating God on earth*
ISBN: 978-1-85345-340-3

**Philemon**
*From slavery to freedom*
ISBN: 978-1-85345-453-0

**Philippians**
*Living for the sake of the gospel*
ISBN: 978-1-85345-421-9

**Prayers of Jesus**
*Hearing His heartbeat*
ISBN: 978-1-85345-647-3

**Proverbs**
*Living a life of wisdom*
ISBN: 978-1-85345-373-1

**Psalms**
*Songs of life*
ISBN: 978-1-78951-240-3

**Revelation 1-3**
*Christ's call to the Church*
ISBN: 978-1-85345-461-5

**Revelation 4-22**
*The Lamb wins! Christ's final victory*
ISBN: 978-1-85345-411-0

**Rivers of Justice**
*Responding to God's call to righteousness today*
ISBN: 978-1-85345-339-7

**Ruth**
*Loving kindness in action*
ISBN: 978-1-85345-231-4

**Song of Songs**
*A celebration of love*
ISBN: 978-1-78259-959-3

**The Armour of God**
*Living in His strength*
ISBN: 978-1-78259-583-0

**The Beatitudes**
*Immersed in the grace of Christ*
ISBN: 978-1-78259-495-6

**The Creed**
*Belief in action*
ISBN: 978-1-78259-202-0

**The Divine Blueprint**
*God's extraordinary power in ordinary lives*
ISBN: 978-1-85345-292-5

**The Holy Spirit**
*Understanding and experiencing Him*
ISBN: 978-1-85345-254-3

**The Image of God**
*His attributes and character*
ISBN: 978-1-85345-228-4

**The Kingdom**
*Studies from Matthew's Gospel*
ISBN: 978-1-85345-251-2

**The Letter to the Colossians**
*In Christ alone*
ISBN: 978-1-855345-405-9

**The Letter to the Romans**
*Good news for everyone*
ISBN: 978-1-85345-250-5

**The Lord's Prayer**
*Praying Jesus' way*
ISBN: 978-1-85345-460-8

**The Prodigal Son**
*Amazing grace*
ISBN: 978-1-85345-412-7

**The Second Coming**
*Living in the light of Jesus' return*
ISBN: 978-1-85345-422-6

**The Sermon on the Mount**
*Life within the new covenant*
ISBN: 978-1-85345-370-0

**Thessalonians**
*Building Church in changing times*
ISBN: 978-1-78259-443-7

**The Ten Commandments**
*Living God's Way*
ISBN: 978-1-85345-593-3

**The Uniqueness of our Faith**
*What makes Christianity distinctive?*
ISBN: 978-1-85345-232-1

For current prices or to order, visit **cwr.org.uk/shop**
Available online or from Christian bookshops.

# Be inspired by God.
# Every day.

Confidently face life's challenges by equipping yourself
daily with God's Word. There is something for everyone...

## Every Day with Jesus

Selwyn Hughes' renowned writing is
updated by Mick Brooks into these
trusted and popular notes.

## Life Every Day

Jeff Lucas helps apply the Bible to
daily life with his trademark
humour and insight.

## Inspiring Women
## Every Day

Encouragement, uplifting scriptures and
insightful daily thoughts for women.

## The Manual

Straight-talking guides to help men
walk daily with God. Written by
Carl Beech.

To find out more about all our daily Bible reading notes, or to take out a subscription,
visit **cwr.org.uk/biblenotes** or call 01252 784700.
Also available in Christian bookshops.

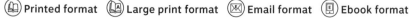 Printed format Large print format Email format Ebook format

# SmallGroup central

*All of our small group ideas and resources in one place*

## Online:

**smallgroupcentral.org.uk**
is filled with free video teaching, tools, articles and a whole host of ideas.

## On the road:

A range of seminars themed for small groups can be brought to your local community. Contact us at **hello@smallgroupcentral.org.uk**

## In print:

Books, study guides and DVDs covering an extensive list of themes, Bible books and life issues.

Find out more at:
**smallgroupcentral.org.uk**

Courses and events

Waverley Abbey College

Publishing and media

Conference facilities

# Transforming lives

CWR's vision is to enable people to experience personal transformation through applying God's Word to their lives and relationships.

Our Bible-based training and resources help people around the world to:
• Grow in their walk with God
• Understand and apply Scripture to their lives
• Resource themselves and their church
• Develop pastoral care and counselling skills
• Train for leadership
• Strengthen relationships, marriage and family life and much more.

**WR** Applying God's Word
to everyday life and relationships

Waverley Abbey House,
rley Lane, Farnham,
y GU9 8EP, UK

ione: +44 (0)1252 784700
info@cwr.org.uk
e: cwr.org.uk

red Charity No. 294387
y Registration No. 1990308

Our insightful writers provide daily Bible reading notes and other resources for all ages, and our experienced course designers and presenters have gained an international reputation for excellence and effectiveness.

CWR's Training and Conference Centre in Surrey, England, provides excellent facilities in an idyllic setting – ideal for both learning and spiritual refreshment.